T0131972

THE Poetry OF Life

FINDING LOVE
THE JESUS WAY

C in Dys

WestBow Press books may be ordered through booksellers or by contacting:

WestBow Press
A Division of Thomas Nelson & Zondervan
1663 Liberty Drive
Bloomington, IN 47403
www.westbowpress.com
844-714-3454

Because of the dynamic nature of the Internet, any web addresses or links contained in this book may have changed since publication and may no longer be valid. The views expressed in this work are solely those of the author and do not necessarily reflect the views of the publisher, and the publisher hereby disclaims any responsibility for them.

Any people depicted in stock imagery provided by Getty Images are models, and such images are being used for illustrative purposes only.
Certain stock imagery © Getty Images.

ISBN: 978-1-9736-9904-0 (sc)
ISBN: 978-1-9736-9906-4 (hc)
ISBN: 978-1-9736-9905-7 (e)

Library of Congress Control Number: 2023909673

Print information available on the last page.

WestBow Press rev. date: 11/07/2023

Foreword

Thanks for the prayers and cooperation of
friends and family in this work.
I believe
these poems and verses
are inspired by the Lord
When we lived for nearly nine years
in the Southern Andes Mountains
with my late then husband
and four children,
We experienced the
miraculous birth of our two sons
in that hazardous, situation.
Also I remember seeing the life of a tiny
bird flicker out, as I tried to save it.
What came to mind at this time
was,
'There's a miracle in movement
that defies the mind of man'.
I pray these poems and verses
help you to trust our miracle working
God through
The Romance that our life is
in the world.

I used to sing a sad song
A lack-love
Song of woe
I went about my duties
<u>because he</u>
told me to.
I thought that life
Was meaningless
With nothing
to rejoice in
till I met you
my darling love
and want to be your wife,
oh yes, I want to be your wife, I do

So, come to me my darling,
come to me my wife
one I'll love for ever, for ever in this life.
One man, one wife.
one love, through life.

Life is a strange thing
with its ups and downs,
Its laughter and tears its
joys and its frowns.
But over all seasons
spring winter; ice snow,
bountiful beauty
is seen by those who know.

Airplane flown by son's father.'Pilot for Life'

My Daddies the PILOT
My daddy is the pilot
in the ups and downs of life
He knows the way before me
though the clouds may hide my view
Those who are around me
are panicking it's true
but I have peace and joy
For HE will take me through.

Life is a bumpy journey

life is a journey with bumps in the road;
we don't know the future
we would if we could
know we'd be happy
with everything good.
But that can't be the case,
the road is so wide,
and many a driver is angry inside
and shouts at you loudly
if you drive too slow.

So, make sure your journey
goes the right way.
Look for the straight road,
that narrow way.
It's not crowded like the other,
people quarrelling and lost,
It's the way of peace and truth,
whatever the cost.
The bumps may be hard
and the journey be long,
but face it with courage
and <u>Victory song.</u>

<u>Time is a created thing</u>
designed for you and me.
A time to live a time to die,
not so eternity;
time is running out it's true

and precious are our days, so let's get up
and do **our best, before it is too late.**

Family singing together 'Songs of Life'.

The wind has had some fun today,
bustling around as children play
leaves are hustling around
up and down.
Pushing the twigs
with crackling sound.
Puddles are bright
with sunshine now,
when a moment ago
rain splattered down
drip drops
sprinkling everywhere
in your eyes and in your hair.
A moment ago
the ground was dry
but now it's wet, with puddles of glee,
puddles for splashing you and me.

Should I create

a can of snakes
that turned around and bit me.
I'd kill those snakes
and would not let
my darling son go near them
but unlike us,
the king of kings
created us who bit him;
then sent his son
his only son
and they bit,
and bit
then killed him.

Not only did he love those snakes
he changed them for the better
and took some into heaven with him,
so, they could live for ever.

Snakes Paradise.' from 'death to life'.

SANDS OF TIME

The sands of time are sinking.
Earth, space, nearly done
The things we see,
we'll see no more,
no more the light of sun,
For darkness will inhabit.
Light will be no more,
and goodness it will fade away
Holy Spirit, here no more.
'Work while it is day,
for the night comes
when no man can work.'
another day is done.
That light that shines around us
Is given by the son.
The son of God shines brightly
His day has just begun
The time He has created
moves on, and on and on.
Till one day 'it is finished'
will echo over all,
the pains and cries
of endless wars,
of want, and enterprise.
Greed and pain will feed no more
on other people's crimes.
Love, will be the antidote
and war will be no more.

A Sex Change

If I try to change my sex how stupid that would be! God made you and God made me just as we should be. To interfere with God's great plan, the creator of us all, is like saying to the King of kings why did you make me so? He's the great designer of everything we know. He loves His work, He loves his world, and Oh; how He loves me!

God is good.

The Clone

If I'm the child of science,
who can my parents be,
am I him or am I her,
or them
or am I really me?
No!
I'm just an interesting experiment
upon the inhuman family tree.
Remember Dolly the sheep,
a man made, clone was she,
and she died before her time.
if I'm like her, it seems to me
my life is on the line.
Since God made time
and natural birth
is what He did design,
I'd rather have a Mum and Dad
who see themselves in me.

THE NEW YEAR

This is a year for you and me
A year to fight the fight of faith,
what- ever else we see.
Those around are fretting
because of Covid new
but we are not like them.
You see
For the faith we have
Is free
We share it with
our loved ones.
We have peace and joy.
We share it with
our friends and foes
and every girl and boy
We have joy.

There's a miracle in movement

That defies the mind of man.
Where did that first breath come from?
Where did it all begin?
We try to find an answer,
which really can't be true;
That a great big accident in time
ended up with me and you.
When I have seen an accident,
when someone drops my watch,
my watch it stops, it will not go,
I cannot tell the time,
If I take it to its maker
He'd know what to do,
For he made it in the first place
He'll know what to do.
So, there is an answer
to where we all come from.
The breath of life
Is breathed on us,
Through the maker of our lives
Who chose to make this happen
Through a loving man and wife;

A LOVE SONG

The wheel of birth is a wonder,
A wonder of space and time,
How the wheel of love
Goes around and round
With an eternal rhyme
With laughter love
And changing moods
All come together in time
And children are born
To love and cherish
And also, they love
In their time.

Waves of love
So sweet and pure
the rhythms
the rhythms
divine,
so; come my darling,
come to me my wife,
join me in this love divine.
Make, agape, love divine.

'David against Goliath.'Strong in life'.

David knew that God was great,
much stronger than Goliath;
the giant roared. the stone it soared
and hit him in the forehead.
So; we should stand
defeat bad men
and women when they tempt us.
They like to roar or simper,
and catch us in their trap.
but we know,
that God will save us,
resist Satan,
know you can.
Don't give up,
his roaring
cannot hurt you now.
just know that he's a liar
a coward and a cheat get your stones from Jesus.
He will save you from defeat.

FAITH FOR HEALING

Faith can move mountains.
Mountains of doubt,
Demons are waiting
With sharp pointed teeth
To nip you
and strip you
and give you disease.
We struggle with darkness
and tremble in fear,
not knowing the outcomes
We daren't take the risk
of standing on Jesus'
foundation of faith;

We wriggle, and wobble
and let demons trouble
our spirit of praise.
Listen to Jesus
whatever the cost;
He dwells in our praise.

IT IS FINISHED

In the eyes of eternity
It's finished
it's done..
Done,
The groans of forsaken
by friends and by kin.
But Jesus said;
finished;
finished.
It's done,

Finished
from war and from sin.
The lost tiny babies
who won't
see the sun.
So sad is the world,
so dark is the night,
but Jesus said
"finished
I've put all things right;
that day on the cross
I put it all right
the devil defeated; now all is put right."

God was in our D.N.A
from the time
that we begun.
He doesn't blame us for the fall
since we all "are born in sin"
no doubt the neighbours
criticised, Joseph for his son,
Jesus conceived by Mary,
before the marriage had begun.
But,
they bore the shame
day by day,
God's beloved son,
taking many sons to glory,
The battle had been won.

Hope be our focus.

we mustn't lose hope
though the journey is fearsome
we learn how to cope.
Children around us
are learning each day
"my mother my father
teach me the way
to overcome problems
to learn what to say,
when bullies surround us
and threaten our way.
They prick us and trick us
into going their way.
But we'll be the leader
on that straight
narrow way.

I like Christmas.

The funny hats,
the happy faces,
children laughing,
having races.
Time to hide your phone away,
and see what presents you have today.
Children singing at your door.
Happy carols of long ago,
of Jesus baby in the hay
and angels singing in the sky,
'Jesus, Jesus,
the baby boy.'
Peace on earth,
and constant joy
to those on earth who follow him.
He gave his all and so should we,
if we want to share eternity with Him.

Wrinkles depart.'wrinkles in life'.

I'm not a slave to fashion

Nor do I want to be.
But I'm a slave of Jesus Christ
Lord of land and sea.
I cannot <u>be</u> my Jesus.
The perfect one
You see
He gave his life
For all of us
Yes;
for you and me.

I cannot say I have no sin,
As that's not true you see,
If I say, I have no sin,
the truth is not in me
.(1 John 1 verse 8 NKJV)

The word of God is precious,
Like jewels in the sea,
Sparkling here, and sparkling there,
Giving joy to you and me.
Some day we will be like him
in eternity you see.
The living God
The King of kings.
How wonderful is he.

The romance of life

Life is so precious
romantic;
fulfilling;
If we are walking in love.
Jesus our bride groom,
and we his dear bride.
Filled with his spirit
in him we abide.
The days they fly by us;
Oh, where have they gone?
But; life's end
is in his hand.
The glorious Son

The Drop Slide.

Life is a drop slide
with dangers unknown
we start as a baby
and cry for the moon
we smile and we giggle
and cuddle our mum
she cries and she laughs as we
take our first steps
we fall over and stagger,
and cry for our mum.
Then we eat our dinner
and make such a mess.
We like the sweet food,
it's like mother's breast,
We splash it around us
oh what a mess,
we don't eat much of it;
so the dog has the rest.

As we get older
we want something more.
We look for excitement
we want more and more,
We're at the top of the Drop Slide,
and waiting to fall,
we don't see the danger
until it's too late.
We fall into confusion
our life is a mess.
What is the answer?
In Jesus find rest.

The drop slide.' The dangers in life'.

Wrinkles

your mum she doesn't like wrinkles,
they make you look old they say.
Botox, is better it's better
yes, better;
It helps you prick wrinkles away.
Wrinkles are crafty, however,
though your face may look younger each day,
your purse it gets older,
and your money gets lesser,
goes further and further away.

The trouble with wrinkles,
they come back again,
again, and again and again.
But one day I know,
as part of God's bride,
I'll have no more wrinkles to show.

My aunty, she married a soldier.. 'Marriage for life'

My Aunty

She married a soldier,
at the beginning of world war 2.
they married on one of his furloughs
they knew their love was true.
His rugged face half smiling,
remembering their wedding night;
her picture in his memory
as he went away to fight.
Though she prayed and prayed
for his safety,
one day a message came through;
Like Mary the mother of Jesus,
a sword cut her spirit in two.
She knew before the telegram came
that her dearest had breathed his last;
a torpedo had shattered the boat
he sailed in,
taking the lives of all the crew.
She cried and cried in secret
mourning the love of her life
for her there could be no other,
she would wait to meet him above.

Though she missed him greatly,
she still had plenty to do,
she looked after her mother with cancer,
and worked during daytime for food.
She led a life that was useful,
teaching her nieces like me,
that Jesus always will help us,
in each situation
with truth.

Halloween

I don't like Halloween
The grisly gripes
The bulging eyes,
the evil witches,
I'd like to push
them all in diches
to live among
the jumpy froggies
peeping out all wet
and soggy
frogspawn for their evil dinner.
as they frizzle
thinner, thinner
and disappear for
ever, ever.
They're not clever, clever, clever.
Never, never,

Happy truth

My daughter you're such a good keeper,
honest and faithful and true.
you cook a good dinner,
and as we get thinner
it helps keep the excess away.
You 're loving and giving
truthful and honest
but often truth hurts I must say,
but when you have finished
we know ourselves better
and it helps us keep liars away.

Let Jesus lead

Let Jesus lead you every day;
every day with him.
Away from sinful pleasures
whatever friends may say.
Take up your cross and follow him
who gave to us
his all.
He knew what was ahead of him
yet set his face like flint.
Toughen up,
fearful ones.
Pray to be like him,
The Word of God will strengthen you
evil under Him.
Tempted was
like all of us,
but he did not sin,
look to Him.

The bubbles of childhood
are precious and rare
like the joys of a young man
with the-wife of his care.
Listen to Jesus,
his love's always near,
giving you pleasures
and joys evermore.

Moses by the burning bush.'Angel of life'.

Moses had a fright one day

before his very eyes;
a bush was burning brightly,
red and yellow
blue and white.
the bush began to speak
it seemed
and tell him what to do.
it was an angel burning bright,
dear father what a sight.
"take off your shoes"
the angel said,
"this is holy ground"
the one who speaks to you right now
will tell you what to do."

To Egypt you will have to go
to set my people free,
for they are slaves to evil kings
and cry and cry to me.
You will show them mighty signs
to help their unbelief,
but still they 'll wander round and round,
till their children take their place

and enter in the promised land
saved by grace.

Joseph running from Potipher's wife.'run for your life'!

Joseph was a young man

too young for such a test,
but always he was trusting,
always did his best.
His brothers they were jealous,
they hated him so much,
they threw him in a filthy hole,
told his father he was dead.
They sold him as a slave,
and saw him on his way,
and thought that was the end of him,
and just went on their way.

Joseph sold to Potiphar,
it really wasn't fun,
but he, worked so hard and did his best,
and was treated like a son..
He was a strong and handsome man,
so thought his master's wife;
She pestered him at every turn to sleep
with her it seems,
Till one day she got physical and grabbed him by the coat
and screamed when he refused her,
and went running for the door.
This meant that he was thrown in jail;
But even there he won;
And honoured God like Jesus did
God's only precious son.
So, when we're tempted to do wrong
to steal or cheat or lie,
let's remember Joseph,
and overcome that sin,
let's run!

Printed in the United States
by Baker & Taylor Publisher Services